# NEW Money PLAYBOOK

## By: Andrew Cass & Jeff Lerner

"Unlock The 5 <u>Mission</u>-<u>Critical</u> Steps To Building A Highly Lucrative, Part Time Internet Business From The Comfort Of Your Home"

*(even if you hate technology!)*

# Table of Contents

# Part 1 - A New Underground World

*By: Andrew Cass*

What if I told you there is a new, different and unusual way to make big money, long-term, leveraging the awesome power of the Internet?

But it's not what you think. No get-rich-quick, MLM, or fly-by-night business model here. What you are about to see is a system that's <u>never</u> been seen by most Entrepreneurs and Business Owners.

But isn't that usually how it goes? The most lucrative wealth building strategies and business models in the world are usually kept from the masses.

But are they really *kept* from the masses? Or

do the masses just not *take the time* to observe and dig deep below the surface to find the true gold?

I say it's the former.

So it's no wonder to us why so many fail when they set out to start an Internet Business. This never has to be the case for you *after* you read this Playbook cover to cover. That's a promise.

Quick back story…

I got my start as an Internet Entrepreneur in 2005 before Google was a search engine, before Facebook was an idea, and before online video even existed. In other words, I've seen it all. I'm a grizzled Veteran.

I feel the need to tell you this because there are so many here-today-gone-tomorrow Experts (so called) teaching success these days. Especially on the Internet.

Very few have the track record that Jeff and I have when it comes to starting, building and scaling businesses to 7-figures, 8-figures and beyond. Combined, we have about 25 years of

Internet Business experience and we've grown five different online businesses <u>from scratch</u> to the 7-figure level and beyond. We are both published authors, pretty good speakers, and we host a cutting-edge Internet TV Show and Podcast called, *"The Success Lab."*

So, it goes without saying that we are <u>more than qualified</u> to deliver you this *New Money Playbook*, which will now serve as your go-to guide when analyzing and selecting the right Internet business model for you for the new and ever-changing Digital Economy we now live in.

Do yourself a favor, don't skim through this Playbook. Read it closely, take notes, and write down questions you have because our team of hand-selected Internet Business Coaches are standing by ready to mentor and advise our readers of our *New Money Playbook* (you!).

In fact, if you're hungry, determined and serious about starting and growing a lucrative Internet business right away, right from the comfort of your home, you can jump the line and apply to work with Jeff and I and our amazing team now by visiting the following link:

**www.MyLifestyleUpgrade.com**

Here's a quick word from one of our members <u>on the next page</u>"....

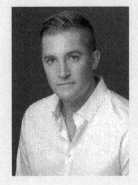

"*I've struggled to generate income in the online business space for the past 6 years and I've never been able to build, produce or sell an online digital product, until I linked up with this team. I started in January of 2017. In that time span, not only have I generated my first commissions online, I am working with them to create my very first digital product that I can market online. Not to mention, the professionally produced videos they're producing for me to go along with my online product so that I can take my personal brand to the next level. They have given me the platform to learn while I earn. This is the vehicle in which I will be able to spread my wings and transcend from being a Struggling Wantrepreneur to Professional Entrepreneur. Thanks guys!*"

**– Lloyd Nolan**

**Now, let's dig into <u>your</u> *New Money Playbook*...**

# Part 2: An Unusual Money-Making System

*By: Jeff Lerner*

I just want to say that I am so happy and excited to be able to share this information with you here and to be able to share some of the insight I've gained over close to a DECADE of doing business online…

Now, you're probably wondering, "Who is this Jeff Lerner guy, and what exactly does he know about earning a full-time income online?"

So let me tell you a little bit about me and my story…

I've been teaching people how to master the business fundamentals necessary to earn a life-changing, full-time income online since 2009.

My mission is to help the people I work with build their business to a level that they can actually retire on. I'm talking about a sustainable, long-term, and highly profitable business that works even when you don't.

But…

As great as all that sounds, the fact is that my career in business sure as heck didn't start out that way. Because I had to learn some hard lessons about the way business really works before I was able to find real success.

But in the process, I discovered just how and why online businesses have made it easier than <u>ever</u> before for any dedicated person to earn a full-time income online.

Now before I get into the specifics, I want to talk about the FRANCHISE business model for a second, a business model just about everyone is familiar with…

McDonald's, Subway…

These businesses are FRANCHISE businesses. That means they allow people to license their business model and open their own franchise location by paying a 'franchising fee' and sharing a percentage of their revenue in what's called a royalty. And in return, the FRANCHISOR provides everything that person, the FRANCHISEE needs to success.

The McDonald's or the Subway, these guys provide the actual business model and the Operations Manual, which is basically the step-by-step specifics of how to run the business. And in return, the franchise owner pays a licensing or franchise fee to "buy in" to the business, and then pays them a percentage of revenue, royalties, for as long as they're in business.

Now, it's important for you to understand that the franchise model brings some <u>immense</u> benefits to the table. You see, the <u>proven</u> aspect of the business model reduces the learning curve significantly. There's absolutely NO testing or experimentation that needs to be done, because everything to do with the business has already been figured out.

This means the business owner, or the franchisee, can get things up and running quickly, because all they have to provide is the money. In return, they get a step-by-step breakdown of how to hire people, where to order their inventory from, what to offer on the menu, how to price their offerings, how to market themselves, etc.

These franchises have proven to be extremely profitable for a very long time, which is why businesses like Subway and McDonald's can charge anywhere from $300,000 to upwards of a Million dollars or more to own one of these businesses. Because they know that, once they hand you the keys, much of the hard work and infrastructure build out is already done.

And here's the best part…

They're always invested in your success, because after your franchise is up and running, you're going to be sharing royalties with them. The franchisor wants to see you succeed, because the more successful you are, the bigger their royalty checks are. So they're going to do a LOT of heavy lifting when it comes to getting your business to run properly and turn a profit.

You can think about it this way: A franchise business is literally a 'business-in-a-box', and about as close as it gets to a sure thing...

Does that make sense?

Are you all following along with me on this?

Do you see why franchise businesses are so profitable?

Now, we're going to move on and come back to me and my story. And to do that, we have to rewind back to the year 2007. That year, I decided that I wanted to open up a Pita Sandwich shop. And this business was going to be a franchise, which means that I had to come up with the money to pay for the 'franchising fee'.

Now, something you may not realize is that, while banks are usually very skeptical about lending large amounts of money to first-time entrepreneurs. They are often very open to lending money to someone who's opening a franchise?

Do you know why?

It's because they know the franchisor, the McDonald's or the Subway, is going to do a lot of the heavy lifting to ensure the franchise is successful, like we said before, right? That means that the business owner is probably going to have NO trouble paying back their loan…

Makes sense, right?

And now the banks are smart, they know a good bet from a bad one. And they don't like to lend money to people that they don't think will be able to pay back that money, which is why they're very selective about lending hundreds of thousands of dollars to someone.

But, because I was opening a franchise, the bank was happy to lend me the $300,000 I needed to open my pita sandwich shop.

Now, we've talked about the franchising fee, but there's a lot more to starting a franchise than just the fee. I also had to deal with my "hard costs."

These are things like…

- Employees
- Insurance
- Rent
- Utilities
- Food Items
- Etc.

And in my case, the hard costs of operating my pita sandwich shop were $30,000 a month. So, that means I needed to make $30,000 in sales <u>every single month</u> just to cover my expenses. And then when you factor in the royalties I had to pay to the franchisor, along with other types of expenses — **only about 50%** of what I made over $30,000 was actual profit.

Hard to believe, right?

I know it is, but trust me, it's the truth, and it's why a traditional brick-and-mortar business is a lot riskier than most people realize. Now, coming back to my pita shop - that means that if I brought in $40,000 in gross monthly income, I only took home about $5,000.

$30,000 of that $40,000 was just to break even. And then 50% of what I made on top of that went to royalties and other costs. Leaving me with just $5,000.

Now I want you to think about something else…

When you're selling $4 to $5 pita sandwiches, and maybe getting an extra buck for chips and a drink, how many sandwiches do you think it takes to generate $40,000 in income?

The answer… is a LOT of sandwiches! And the truth is, selling those $4 to $5 sandwiches is not even where I made most of my money. You see, where I made my money was in **high-ticket CATERING sales.**

Local corporate businesses would hire us to cater their events and business functions and this allowed my pita sandwich shop to make some higher-ticket sales of several thousand dollars apiece, which went a long way towards paying all of the business's hard costs and the interest on my bank loan.

Look, the truth is that NO business can count on low-ticket, front-end sales to make large scale profits. It's just NOT possible. You need higher-ticket sales to generate large scale, life-changing profits which is why, when the economic crash hit in 2008, I lost everything.

But here's the thing: It wasn't because people stopped buying pita sandwiches. It was because all the local corporations we were catering for, or in other words, all of our high-ticket customers, got hit hard…

They started laying off employees, and they <u>stopped</u> paying for catered food at their events. I had lost my high-ticket back-end piece of my business.

And here's the lesson, and it's true of most business models, including the so-called "sure thing" franchise business models…

Your front end, lower cost sales will pay most of your bills. Most, but not all. To pay the last bit of your hard costs and actually make any money as the owner, you have to have back-end, higher value sales. Even though I was still selling hundreds of $4 sandwiches a day without the back-end, I couldn't keep up and it wasn't long before I missed the first lease payment. And in less time than it took to even get my business started, I defaulted on my bank loan and lost the business.

The bank seized all my assets, froze all my accounts, and basically crushed my entire business in the blink of an eye. At the end of it all, I had nothing left but a little bit of cash I had sitting in the store safe. So I took that home in a paper bag, and as soon as I got home, I started searching online for NEW and DIFFERENT options.

And as it turns out, I was about to get really lucky because while I was searching online, I came across some incredible business training that offered the potential to make some good money promoting it. The only thing was... I was going to have to dump every dollar I had left into advertising for this new business if I was going to have any chance at succeeding. So I swallowed my pride, did my best to quell the butterflies, and I took the plunge.

Looking back, it was a gamble that changed my life forever. It was in my 1st month promoting this business training that I made my first $1,000 online, and after that, things were never the same. This was also the business where I met my Co-Author of this Playbook and my Partner, Andrew Cass.

I made more profit in ONE DAY than I had made in an entire MONTH in my brick and mortar business!

My 2nd month I made a little over $2,000...
My 3rd month I made a little over $4,000...

And by the end of my first year, I had made over $400,000, which allowed me to square away all my debts from my brick-and-mortar franchise.

The next year, I went on to hit 7-figures in income because I followed the system diligently and daily, and in return, the system rewarded me handsomely for my hard work...

I had gone from being $400,000+ in debt with NO idea what to do, to making 7-figures online two years later.

Amazing, right?

Have you ever experienced similar, hard financial struggles?

Wouldn't it be incredible to be able to turn that around and start earning a 6 or 7-figure income online in less than two years?

It would be, right?

If you think that sounds exciting, read on...
I can tell you from experience it is incredible, and it's <u>very</u> possible. So in parting let me just say this...

What you're about to learn here <u>WILL</u> change your life…

How do I know?

Because it not only happened for me, but I've seen it happen time and time again with some of the people Andrew and I work with. When people start to master these essential skills, and leverage these **5 key "Mission Critical" steps** that you're about to learn, they go on start earning a real, full time income online, usually part time.

See what another member, Gerry Kirk, had to say <u>on the next page</u>"….

*"Entrepreneurship is not an easy path. For over a decade, I've tried many things, none which have given me the time freedom, financial stability and world impact I'm seeking. Then along comes a system that takes much of the burden off*  *of my shoulders... This T3FP system, with its high quality traffic offerings, well tested funnels, high ticket commissions and a sales team to close sales means I don't have to be the "expert" at a lot of things anymore. I'm surrounded by people like me, and guided by leadership I trust. I've grown personally by leaps and bounds through their amazing events. That means a lot to me. This is now my home, and I'm here to stay."*

**-Gerry Kirk**

Once you see the pieces of the puzzle and how they fit together, it will makes a lot more sense.

Ok, let's dig into the five Mission-Critical steps. I will call them "Building Blocks" here in the New Money Playbook...

# Building Block #1:

# TRAFFIC

---

No business can survive without traffic. Plain and simple. Now, I want you to think about a traditional brick-and-mortar store for a second, okay?

Everyday someone walks by the store, or has any kind of visual interaction with the store, or with an ad of theirs, this is what's called an "impression." And when someone actually enters the store, that's what's considered a "lead." And leads who purchase become "customers."

Now, online, you get charged for advertising either by IMPRESSIONS or by CLICKS. But no matter which option you choose, your goal is simple: To get as many people, or traffic, into your store as possible, for as little as possible!

Makes sense, right?

You want to get as many people in the door as possible to increase the number of sales you can make, and you want to be getting those people in the door as cheaply as possible. This is how you maximize your profits.

The more traffic you get, the more sales you make. And the less you pay for that traffic, the more you profit. Now, the problem with traffic for a traditional brick-and-mortar store is that you can't necessarily pick-and-choose the kind of traffic you want. Because if you open up a pizza shop in the middle of a corn field in Iowa, well, you're going to get a lot of Farmers (whether you like it or not).

But if you open up a pizza shop in downtown Chicago, now we're talking because your pizza shop in downtown Chicago is going to be a lot more likely to attract a bunch of hungry pizza-lovers because that's exactly where they are - in Chicago!

Traffic for online businesses works differently, and actually gives online business owners a HUGE leg up because we can pick and choose our traffic online. Most online advertising platforms like Facebook, Google, and others, have very complex targeting options that allow you to specify <u>EXACTLY</u> what kind of person you want to "walk in" to your online store…

This leads to a much higher "conversion rate", which is the rate at which you're able to convert impressions (or clicks) into LEADS, and then convert those leads into Customers. And this means more profits for your business, plain and simple.

Do you see how that works?

If you think about it for a second, YOU are actually a perfect example of Building Block #1 in action. You're here reading this book because we wanted passionate and motivated people who are ready to start their own online business so they can earn a life-changing income while providing massive value to the world at the same time. And YOU signed into get this Playbook.

Isn't that cool?

And so that's why the first Building Block behind all of the most lucrative Internet Business models is understanding that <u>NO</u> business can survive without **Traffic.**

# Building Block #2:
# FUNNELS

Alright, we're going to move on to Building Block #2 now, which is that to make "full-time" money online, you must have a high-converting Sales Funnel.

Now, you may be wondering what a Sales Funnel is. First, let me ask you question: Have you ever been to McDonald's to get a hamburger, only to get "upsold" on a fries and a Coke?

THAT is a Sales Funnel. You see, McDonald's hardly makes any profit on that hamburger because they have to pay, on average, $1.91 to get you in the door and the burger only costs $2.09. That's just $0.18 in profit.

But, when they sell you the fries and the coke along with your burger for an extra $1.77, they make an extra $1.32 in profit. That's a total of 8X the profit of the initial sale. And THAT is why you must have a sales funnel in place to make "full-time" money online.

If you only have ONE product to sell, after you recover your advertising costs, you might be surprised to find that there isn't much money left over — this is a giant mistake many, many online Entrepreneurs make.

Here's another way to think about this…

If you only have ONE product to sell to your customers, how can you increase the amount of money your business makes?

There's only one way you can do it — and it's by acquiring more customers.

When a customer comes in and buys the only product you have to sell them, and that's it, then you can't make any more money from that customer. But, if instead you have "multiple" products that are related, that complement each other, that increase or amplify how fast someone can get the results you're promising them, then you can make a lot more money.

There's a **Universal Truth** of marketing and sales that I want to share with you that most people don't realize, and it's this:

It's much easier to sell additional products to an existing customer than it is to sell to a NEW customer for the first time. You may want to read that again.

Can you see the power in this? Do you understand why that is?

It's because your existing customers, the people who have already bought from you, they've already indicated that they **Trust** you. And gaining trust is a very big accomplishment as many fail to do so online today (a huge opportunity).

They trust you enough to pull out their credit card and purchase something from you. They've already been through your sales process, and they're satisfied with what they received, which makes them <u>100 times more likely</u> to buy from you <u>again</u>, compared to someone who has never heard of you or what you're selling.

When you have a high-converting Sales Funnel working for your business, there are actually two more ways you can make more money besides acquiring more customers…

The first, is by increasing how often each customer buys. Instead of buying from you one time and then walking away, you can get your customers to come back again and again to buy from you. That's the first way you can increase how much money you make…

The second, is by increasing how much each customer spends every time they buy from you. How do you do that?

With "upsells." Remember that McDonalds example earlier?

By offering your customers a mix of products at different price points, and gradually making higher and higher-priced offers to customers who continue to buy from you, you can dramatically increase your DPL, which stands for "dollars-per-lead."

(By the way, Amazon is THE master at all of this. Any wonder now why they are one of the richest companies in the world?)

So, just to recap…

If you only sell ONE product, the only way you can increase your income is by acquiring more customers. But if you have a high-converting sales funnel, you can increase it two more ways (three in total):

1.  **Acquiring more customers**

2.  **Increase how often customers buy**

3.  **Increasing how much customers spend each time they buy**

And <u>THE</u> <u>BEST</u> part about Sales Funnels...

On the Internet, Sales Funnels can be 100% "Automated." An online Sales Funnel is an automated process that allows you to turn your leads, people who have indicated they're interested in what you have to offer, into

Customers, and turning those Customers into <u>Repeat</u> <u>Customers</u>.

The operative word here: Automated.

That's the beautiful thing, and it's precisely why this is such an important power of harnessing the Internet to create lifestyle and financial freedom for yourself. Because once you set up a Sales Funnel, it can run completely on its own, which means this entire process of attracting Leads, converting them into Customers, and then convincing them to buy from you again and again, is ALL happening no matter what you happen to be doing…

Let's take a look at what a Sales Funnel actually looks like, so you can understand this is a little better…

First up, we have a "lead Capture" or "Opt-In" web page, where someone provides you with their contact info (Email address or phone number) in exchange for something of value, like a free Book, free video, webinar, etc.

From there, you immediately make them a **high-value, low-ticket** offer…

Now what does that look like?

Well, it depends on what market you're in, but it generally means a product that's under $100. The goal is to create an irresistible offer, something they can't afford to turn down. From there, you continue to make other, complimentary offers at higher and higher price points. Now, the beautiful part about how this works is it allows your customers to UPGRADE their relationship with you at their choosing.

They're essentially self-selecting themselves, because you're getting them to raise their hand each and every time you make them an offer. And every one of those customers who takes advantage of that offer and buys it is raising their hand and saying, "YES! I'd like to receive more value."

Now I hope you haven't forgotten the most important part about all this…

Which is that often times, 100% of this can run on Autopilot. Once you've got your Sales

Funnel set up, it's working for you day and night…

No matter whether you're at the computer, eating, sleeping, traveling, or out just enjoying life. Your Sales Funnel is hard at work converting leads into buyers, and buyers into repeat buyers.

This is critical, because if you want to achieve unlimited lifestyle freedom and earn a life-changing income online, then you need a way to make money regardless of what you're doing in that exact moment. And that's precisely what a great Sales Funnel will do for you. This is exactly how the most successful online businesses work.

Do you see how powerful that is? Can you see how quickly this stuff could change your life? Can you imagine rolling out of bed in the morning, firing up your laptop, and seeing that you made 10, 20, 50, 100, or even 1000 sales overnight, while you were sleeping?

How great would that feel? Amazing, right?

That is what it means to be an Internet Entrepreneur — To own a real business that pays you no matter what you're doing, and whether you're working or not. And if you want to achieve that kind of lifestyle and financial freedom, you've got to create something that will pay you no matter what you're doing.

That's why understanding how a Sales Funnel makes sales for you, almost 100% on autopilot, is so important. I'm sure you're starting to see that now, and understand just how much this stuff can change your life…

# Building Block #3:
# FILTERS

---

B uilding Block #3 is that the best Sales Funnels also act as Filters to keep certain people <u>out</u>…Yes, <u>out</u>.

Now, how does a great Sales Funnel act as a Filter, and why do we want to keep certain people out? For starters, no matter what business you're in, you should know who your IDEAL CUSTOMER is.

This is the person for whom your product or service is custom made for, the person who's going to receive the maximum benefit from your product or service, and the person whose problems are solved by your product or service.

There is an ideal customer for every single business out there, which means that one of the most important goals of your Sales Funnel is to attract as many of those ideal customers as possible. And on the flip side, it must also keep as many NON-IDEAL CUSTOMERS out.

You see, if your Sales Funnel attracts and allows unqualified people, people who are not your ideal customers to pass through, then your business is going to suffer.

Why?

Because these people are not who your products or services are meant for, which means that both parties lose. There is a disconnect. But when your Sales Funnel works properly and prevents these people from passing through, then it ensures that only the right people proceed — Your IDEAL customers.

And this means that, because you're only working with the IDEAL customer for your product or service, you can deliver better results, and your customers are going to be much happier as a result.

You'll be able to collect more testimonials and social proof that demonstrate the power of your product or service. And you'll have the power of **word-of-mouth** working for you too, as happy customers are much more likely to recommend you to their friends, family, and the rest of their extended network.

All of this comes together to mean one thing for your business:

More customers and more profits. Period.

You're doomed without a consistent flow of either.

Now, I mentioned earlier that YOU are a perfect example of our traffic strategies at work. But let's talk about the flipside for a second…

Who are we trying to keep OUT?

Dabblers, Toe-Dippers, and Tire-Kickers.

Why do we want to keep these people out?

Because these folks aren't actually serious about starting their own business. They're people who are not going to take this training seriously then they'll turn around tell everyone who will listen that it doesn't work.

That's who we don't want in any part of our sales funnel, and we design all of our marketing materials specifically to communicate to these people that they're better off going somewhere else, doing something else. Because this does require work. Not nearly as much work as a 9 to 5 job, but anything legitimate and worthwhile requires real work. Don't let anyone tell you different.

Can you now see why you want to keep certain kinds of people OUT of your sales funnel?

---

**NOTE:** Andrew and I recently created an advanced online business model where <u>we build ALL the Sales Funnels and Filters for our members</u> so that they don't get bogged down for months and months on this stuff. We call it the "T3FP Money-Making System." Very awesome, if we do say so ourselves! For a free video tour visit:

**www.MyLifestyleUpgrade.com**

---

# Building Block #4:
# FOLLOW UP

---

You've most likely heard the phrase: "The fortune is in the Follow Up."

Before I dive into this one, I want to ask you something…

When you buy something, what happens?

Think about it…

You get a confirmation or a receipt, you get tracking information if you purchased a physical product, you might get asked to fill out a survey on your experience.

But more importantly, if the business you purchased the product from has a proper sales funnel in place, then you receive information about additional products and services, right? *(Think Amazon).*

Now here's something most people don't realize about doing business online: Almost all higher-ticket sales (which are generally products that are priced above $500) happen <u>after</u> a relationship has been established.

And that's because it takes time to establish trust, which is what you need to sell high-ticket products or services successfully. You need your customers to trust you, and you need to give them some time to "upgrade" their relationship with you one step at a time...

That's why Follow Up is so important for any online business. Because you can't sell someone a $10,000 product on a one-time cold call. But you can sell someone a $10,000 product when they:

- Have purchased something from you already and had a positive buying experience

- Feel like they actually got what they paid for

- Have been educated on why your $10,000 option may be exactly what they need

Once you've built up rapport and trust with somebody, and you've shown them that you do actually have their best interests at heart, then they will be happy to buy a product that costs $10,000 or more from you.

The reason that the Fortune is in well-executed Follow Up is because the real profits aren't in the first sale you make to a customer, they're in the 2nd, 3rd, and 4th sales of higher-ticket products that come <u>after</u> the relationship has been established.

And when you have a perfect blend of lower-ticket and higher-ticket products combined with great Follow Up, your potential to generate sales and high revenue is practically limitless.

Can you see why you have to put the work in and Follow Up with someone via email, regular mail, and over the phone before you can sell them a $10,000 or a $20,000+ product or service? Can you start to see just how powerful the right follow-up can be?

We've now covered four out of our five "Building Blocks" already, which means that it's time for the fifth and final one...

# Building Block #5:
# PRODUCT MIX

---

The most successful businesses in the world all leverage a <u>proven</u> Product Mix, a portfolio of lower priced **and** higher priced products and services to maximize their profits.

Hopefully by now you're starting to see how this all comes together…

To understand why the most successful businesses need to leverage a proven Product Mix to maximize their profits, we're going to do a little crash course on traditional "Affiliate Marketing."

I say, "traditional" because there is non-traditional, highly-lucrative type of Affiliate

Marketing (that very few are aware of) which is how Andrew and I got our start online long ago.

Affiliate Marketing tends to be a launching pad for many, many 7-Figure Internet Entrepreneurs. It was for both of us. It is, by far, the fastest and easiest way to make real money, fast on the Internet <u>without</u> having to create <u>ANY</u> of your own products. Yes, you read that correctly.

But… Only when one graduates (so to speak) to the non-traditional, highly-lucrative side of Affiliate Marketing, which we'll talk about later on in this Playbook.

Pay close attention…

Traditional Affiliate Marketing works like this:

A product creator or product owner wants to make more sales of his existing products and services. So to do that, he offers to pay AFFILIATES a commission for any sales they make of his product.

And just to be clear: the term 'Affiliates' just refers to anyone who's willing to sell the product in question…

So the way it works is like this:

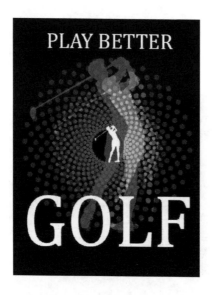

Let's say you sign up as an Affiliate to promote an eBook on how to improve your golf swing. The creator of the eBook offers to pay you a commission for each sale you make of his eBook. And to track your sales, you get an Affiliate Link with a tracking ID that is unique to you.

He supplies the PRODUCT and you supply the TRAFFIC. And when a sale is made to someone that you sent to that offer via your Affiliate link, you generate a commission.

Simple, right?

It saves you <u>a ton of time and aggravation</u> from having to create your own products and build out your own sales funnel.

(As an example, Amazon has one of the largest Affiliate Partner networks in the world. They have, literally, Millions of Affiliates selling products and services on the Amazon platform and sharing in the profits with Amazon.)

But here's the thing…

We know now from this Playbook that the <u>real</u> <u>profits</u> in the most successful business models are in the back-end, in making <u>repeat</u> sales to <u>existing</u> customers by offering them higher priced products than the initial offer that got them in the door.

So think about this for a second…

You as the Affiliate are doing all the legwork, all the heavy lifting, to find the people and drive traffic to this person's offer. In return, you're paid a commission for each sale. If we're talking about an eBook that costs $19.95, then you could expect to be paid at least $10 for each sale you make, which is basically a commission rate of 50%.

If you're making $10 per sale of this eBook, how many sales is it going to take for you to earn say $5,000 a month? Well, if you're only making $10 a sale, you'd need to make 500 sales <u>every</u> <u>month</u> just to earn $5,000 in monthly income. And that is a LOT of sales. That's 500 brand new customers you're creating each and every month.

Even if you were getting 5x as much per sale, even if you were making $50 per sale, you'd still need to make 100 sales every month just to make $5,000.

And guess what?

In the meantime, you're handing off customers over to the product creator, customers who are possibly going to go on to spend hundreds or even thousands of dollars in repeat purchases after the initial sale. And what cut are you getting of those subsequent, repeat purchases?

Zero.

You're not seeing any of those **Back-End Profits** we discussed earlier.

And let's not forget that driving traffic has a cost (which you can do through free channels like social media, but in this case you'd most likely be running paid advertisements).

So when you factor those expenses into your tiny slice of the pie, it becomes pretty clear that you're really getting the short end of the stick here, doesn't it?

Can you see how this traditional, Low-Ticket Affiliate Marketing model makes it incredibly difficult to earn any real money and generate a full time income online?

By the way, this is how the great majority of traditional brick-and-mortar businesses operate as well. They typically have ONE small to medium-sized product offering and they bet the farm on doing enough volume to make a profit. Stressful, to say the least.

Think about a restaurant…

90% of them begin and end with the "hope" that enough customers come in the door each day and buy a meal for maybe $50 to $150. That's it. That's the whole business model for most! No back end, no real sales process or upsell process past the waiter at the table and very little, if any, follow up. It's no wonder 90% go out of business, right?

This example demonstrates why the most successful businesses leverage a proven Product Mix, a product mix that includes a blend of lower-ticket <u>AND</u> higher-ticket products that allows them to maximize the value of each and every customer that comes through the door. Because it allows them to get as many people in the door with an irresistible, low-ticket but extremely high value offer. And then builds on the trust and rapport that is established by that initial purchase, by offering higher-ticket offerings that generate way more profit for everybody involved, from the affiliates to the product creator or business owner.

Now can you imagine how long it would take you to build up to the point where you're making $5,000 every month in a traditional Affiliate Marketing business?

What about $10,000 a month? Or $50,000 a month?

It would take forever. Because how are you supposed to reach those income levels when you're only making $10 or $20 a sale, and you're not getting a piece of any of those lucrative, back-end commissions?

The answer, which is clear to you by now I'm sure, is with **High Ticket** or sometimes called, **Top-Tier Affiliate Marketing.**

In contrast to the traditional low-ticket model, high-ticket Affiliate Marketing involves promoting incredibly well-packaged, high value offers that sell for $5,000, $10,000, $20,000, or even more.

All of a sudden your 50% commission rate goes from being worth $10 a sale to being worth $5,000 or $10,000 a sale. Now that's real money.

Imagine if you were able to make a $5,000 to $10,000 commission off of a single sale? Imagine if you could even just make $1,000 a sale?

Can you see how quickly your income would grow if you were making that much for every affiliate sale you made?

And here's the best part:

With a high-ticket Affiliate Marketing business model, you can position yourself to earn a commission on <u>every</u> sale that is made to your leads — including on the back-end!

This means that each and every lead you generate could be worth $1,000, $5,000, or even $10,000+ to you. Because you're getting a commission off of all the BACK END purchases they make, even after you've been paid a commission for their INITIAL purchase...

As you can see it's a totally different ball game once you "graduate" to the non-traditional, high-ticket Affiliate Marketing model.

And the best part…

The best high-ticket Affiliate Marketing systems out there literally invest <u>tens of thousands of dollars</u> in split-testing to make sure that every single step of their **Sales Funnel** and **Filters** are converting well and actually producing results. And that includes hiring expert phone sales teams to make those follow-up phone calls, develop those relationships, and convert those leads into high-ticket sales.

This is <u>exactly</u> the model Andrew and I created for the right type of Entrepreneurs (most likely YOU, if you're still reading this right now). We've essentially built a Top-Tier Affiliate Marketing business model that <u>perfectly</u> encompasses ALL five Building Blocks you've read about here in the **New Money Playbook.** And we meticulously tested ALL aspects of it before rolling it out, based on our 30+ years of Online Business and Internet Marketing experience. Details at:

**www.MyLifestyleUpgrade.com**

So think about this for a second…

Imagine if you positioned yourself to become part of a high-ticket Affiliate Marketing system that leveraged a <u>proven</u> Product Mix in combination with a fully split-tested, high-converting Sales Funnel that also included expert phone sales people who essentially do ALL of the selling for you. And instead of every sale being worth $10 or $20 to you, each sale is worth $1,000, $5,000 or even $10,000+ to you.

And instead of having to do all the legwork and all the heavy lifting to actually find new customers, only to watch the product creator collect all the backend profits, you got a slice of all those back-end profits too.

Can you imagine how great that would be? Can you imagine generating one single lead who, for example, went on to buy a $2,500 product, a $5,000 product, a $10,000 product, and even a $20,000 product over a period of time? That would be almost $20,000 to in commissions to you — all from ONE single lead!

Remember: you're doing the <u>exact</u> same amount of work as with traditional, low-ticket Affiliate Marketing. But instead, you're making way more money over a longer period of time…

The potential is enormous. And the amount of people looking for an Internet Business model like this is even bigger, and growing each and every day by leaps and bounds, as more and more smart, sophisticated, Entrepreneurs are looking for additional income streams.

Let me tell you this, the feeling of waking up in the morning and opening an Email alerting you that you just made a $1,000, $5,000 or $10,000 commission and that the money is on the way to you by direct deposit, is amazing.

Life-changing for many, to say the least.

One of our amazing members, Michelle Lopez agrees.  See her story <u>on the next page</u>…

*"I've worked with other companies that offer an online affiliate marketing business model but nothing even comes close in comparison to this! A done-for-you business that truly embodies The Ultimate Laptop Lifestyle! The one-on-one coaching & mentorship is like nothing I've ever experienced. I've never worked in an industry where I felt so completely supported. The best part of this community is the people. The positive, creative energy they all exude is highly contagious. This isn't a community--we're a family. A family whose sole purpose is to see others in the best light possible & lift them up."*

**- Michelle Lopez**

# Part 3 - A Lifestyle Upgrade

*By: Andrew Cass & Jeff Lerner*

The 5 "Building Blocks" that we've just shared with you are the heart and soul of every <u>ultra-successful</u> business, both online and offline. But it works best online due to the leverage and automation the Internet provides a business today.

As mentioned earlier, in our organization, we call it the **The T3FP Money-Making System.** As you now know, it stands for:

- Traffic
- Funnels
- Filters
- Follow-Up
- Product Mix

Now that you've learned just how powerful this system can be when it's applied properly by those who fully understand it, you have a <u>very</u> <u>serious</u> advantage. Actually, you have an Unfair Advantage. We mean that.

This crash course is, literally, the foundation education that very few get and it's a BIG reason why so many struggle with online businesses today. But, you won't ever have to because we have a special invitation for you that, if you accept, will catapult your success online faster than anything we've ever seen.

If you're ready to upgrade your lifestyle we want show you these 5 Mission-Critical steps **in action** and how they can work for you to <u>dramatically</u> increase your monthly cash flow. This is an unusual chance for you to leverage a <u>proven</u> business model that we've spent years perfecting so that you can start earning life-changing income immediately.

And it all starts with our proprietary **"16 Steps to 6-Figures"** Advanced Training with Live Coaching. Yes, with <u>real</u> humans walking you through each and every step so that no stone is left unturned, so that you can get on the fast track to making The T3FP

Money-Making System generate incredible income for YOU and your family as well.

Consider this training New Money Playbook on Steroids. Or, think of New Money Playbook as college football and 16 Steps to 6-Figures as the National Football League (professional football). In other words, this is a giant leap up from here.

It is by Application Only. We invite you to step up and apply at:

**www.MyLifestyleUpgrade.com**

As the saying goes, "knowledge is power."

But, that's really only half true…

Knowledge is <u>potential</u> power. It only becomes <u>real</u> power with clear direction and implementation. And it is that direction that we, along with our amazing team of Coaches and Support Staff can give you through the "16 Steps to 6-Figures" training system.

Just one final **Warning** before we part…

Upgrading one's lifestyle, personally and professionally, can often be uncomfortable, initially. However, those who push through a bit of discomfort ultimately get exposed to options and luxuries very few ever see, which leads to Freedom and Control, something very few have.

Go boldly my friend. We hope to see you on the other side…

Andrew Cass & Jeff Lerner

*" In my 16 years online, this is the most impactful online business I have been a part of. Not only is it the most lucrative, it is also focused on what matters most --*

*Developing people to be the biggest and best versions of themselves. The money is great, yes, but who we become along the way is much more important and this community we have here is the greatest catalyst in taking one from average, to good, to great. I've found a great home and I am grateful to be here."*

**- Cory Reynolds**

"*I've tried many different types of online businesses over the years and I always felt very alone building my business. Plugging into this system allowed me to leverage other people's success stories as well as their professionally designed sales funnels, follow up processes and even their exclusive traffic relationships to take my own business to a whole new level. The training programs and live events have helped me to grow my skills and my results as a marketer and entrepreneur and their leadership team and supportive community has been there for me every step of the way.*"

**- Adam Chandler**

Disclaimer:

While we make every attempt to properly and accurately report success and/or income testimonials, these stories are no guarantee of future results or income. All featured members have followed complete training and business marketing steps that are available inside the 16 Steps To 6-Figures training, and often go above and beyond to grow their marketing and personal brand.